Venus

Earth

Saturn

Asteroid Belt

Neptune

A Look at Saturn

A Look at Saturn

Ray Spangenburg and Kit Moser

Franklin Watts

A DIVISION OF SCHOLASTIC INC.
NEW YORK · TORONTO · LONDON · AUCKLAND
SYDNEY · MEXICO CITY · NEW DELHI · HONG KONG
DANBURY, CONNECTICUT

For
HEATHER AND LYNN
forthright and rich
in wisdom

Photographs ©: Art Resource, NY/Scala: 19; Athéna Coustenis/DESPA/Paris-Meudon Observatory: 82; Bridgeman Art Library International Ltd., London/New York/Private Collection: 18 (EDI32167); Calvin J. Hamilton: 54 (raw Voyager data courtesy of NASA); Corbis Sygma: 24 (T. Campion), 88 (Tony Korody); Corbis-Bettmann: 21, 50; Courtesy of Linda Spilker: 32; Finley-Holiday Films: 45, 46, 65, 81 (JPL), 2, 63, 100; Liaison Agency, Inc.: 31 (M. Brown/Florida Today), 30, 99 (Gamma Pologne); NASA: 56 (NSSDC/GSFC), 66, 71 (JPL/David Seal), 8, 22, 37, 44; National Geographic Image Collection/William H. Bond: 61; Photo Researchers, NY: 11 (Julian Baum/SPL), 55 (Chris Butler/SPL), 39 (Lynette Cook/SPL), 84, 89, 104 (David Ducros/SPL), 14, 15 (David A. Hardy/SPL), 41 (NASA/SPL), cover (NASA/SS) 53 (Ludek Pesek/SPL), 13, 38, 49, 94, 109 (Space Telescope Science Institute/NASA/SPL), 20, 59, 79 (SPL), 77 (Detlev Van Ravenswaay/SPL); Photri: 25, 27, 29, 35, 36, 67, 68, 69, 70, 110; The Planetary System: 51.

The photograph on the cover shows Saturn and some of its moons. *Voyager 2* captured the image opposite the title page. It shows a false-color image of Saturn's B and C rings.

Library of Congress Cataloging-in-Publication Data

Spangenburg, Ray.
    A look at Saturn / by Ray Spangenburg and Kit Moser.
        p. cm.—(Out of this world)
    Includes bibliographical references and index.
    ISBN 0-531-11770-7 (lib. bdg.) 0-531-16564-7 (pbk.)
       1. Saturn (Planet)—Juvenile literature. [1. Saturn (Planet)] 1.Moser, Diane, 1944-
II. Title. III. Out of this world (Franklin Watts, Inc.)

QB671 .S59   2001
523.46—dc 21   00-051356

Acknowledgments

To all those who have contributed to *A Look at Saturn,* we would like to take this opportunity to say thank you. Especially, a word of appreciation to our editor, Melissa Stewart, whose steady flow of creativity, energy, enthusiasm, and dedication have infused this entire series. We would also like to thank Sam Storch, Lecturer at the American Museum-Hayden Planetarium, who reviewed the manuscript and made many insightful suggestions. Finally, to Tony Reichhardt and John Rhea, once our editors at the former *Space World* magazine, thank you for starting us out on the fascinating journey that we have taken—to Saturn and many other places—during our years of writing about space.

Contents

In 1980, the spacecraft *Voyager 1* visited Saturn. It captured this image of the great ringed planet and three of its moons—Tethys (outer left), Enceladus (inner left), and Mimas (right).

Saturn
Close Up

Saturn is a huge, butterscotch-colored globe of gas—a vast, swirling world with no surface. No space travelers or astronaut explorers will ever "land" on Saturn. The planet has no mountains or valleys and no rivers or streams. Nevertheless, Saturn is a fascinating place. It is surrounded by seven rings and an enormous family of moons—at least eighteen, and possibly as many as thirty. Some are very small, but all are solid and offer potential landing sites for visiting astronauts. Just imagine what it would be like for an astronaut to touch down on a world so close to Saturn's golden glow and ringed beauty. Saturn is the second-largest planet in the solar system, and one of the most intriguing.

Some of Saturn's moons travel inside the planet's rings. Standing on the surface of one of these moons as it travels around the dark side of Saturn, a visiting astronaut looks out at the nighttime sky toward the big planet. There she sees an enormous object with rounded boundaries hovering overhead. Cutting across the planet, the eerily sunlit edge of Saturn's rings casts a faint light on the planet's darkened cloud tops. No stars shine in this region of the sky—they are blocked by the planet's huge shape. A sprinkling of starlight around the edges of the massive planet remind the astronaut of the presence of the vast and distant universe.

A second astronaut rambles about on the sunlit surface of another moon that travels inside Saturn's rings. He stands with Saturn at his back, looking toward the Sun. This view shows the band of shadow cast by Saturn's rings as they cut across the distant Sun. This same band shades the smooth *craters* of the little moon. A portion of the rings always intervenes between the small moon and the Sun.

Next, the astronauts hike among the chunks of icy rock that orbit in jumbled but orderly rings around the great planet's equator. Using jetpacks strapped on their backs, the visitors zoom from one rocky chunk to another, dodging through the mist of granules and pebbles between the larger chunks. All the while, Saturn's golden globe glimmers as it reflects the Sun's bright light.

It will be many, many years before such an imaginary voyage becomes a reality. For now, scientists must study the ringed planet from afar. Fortunately, data and photos gathered by equipment on Earth and devices aboard robotic spacecraft have taught us a great deal about Saturn. Using that information, this book will take you on an

Saturn's gassy globe has no surface, so astronauts will never land there. However, they could visit some of the large chunks that make up the planet's rings.

extraordinary, fact-filled journey to Saturn. You will have a chance to plunge through the planet's many layers of clouds and explore its inner dynamics. You will also learn about the fascinating rings and moons that constantly circle Saturn—the queen of the planets.

Chapter 1

The Great Ringed World

Like a jewel in the night sky, Saturn's pale yellow sphere is surrounded by elegant and complex rings that shimmer in the sunlight. Even through a backyard telescope, Saturn is breathtaking. Encircled by its beautiful and mysterious rings, Saturn is one of the most impressive objects in the outer solar system.

Scientists classify Saturn as a gas giant. Jupiter, Uranus, and Neptune are also gas giants. All these planets are composed mainly of hydrogen and helium—two lightweight elements that usually exist as gases. They began to form about 4.6 billion years ago when a vast cloud of whirling dust and gas began to collapse and condense into a huge, flattened disk called a *nebula*.

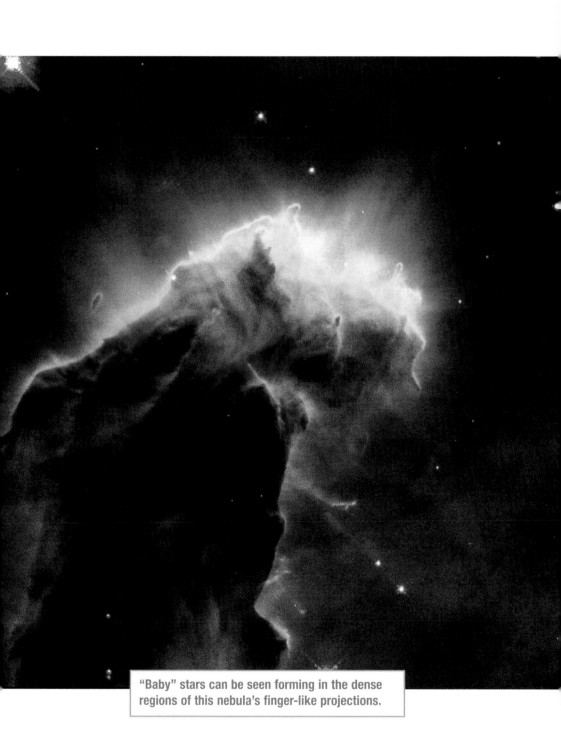

"Baby" stars can be seen forming in the dense regions of this nebula's finger-like projections.

At the center of this rapidly collapsing material, the temperature became so high that *nuclear fusion* began to take place. In this reaction, hydrogen gas was converted to helium gas and enormous quantities of energy were released into space. A new star was born, and that star was our Sun.

As shown in this artwork, the solar system began as a disk-shaped nebula. The Sun, planets, moons, asteroids, and comets all formed from this mass of dust and gases.

At almost the same time, smaller clumps of material formed from the nebula. These clumps were not big enough to become stars, so they condensed into *planetesimals*—the beginnings of what eventually became the group of planets, moons, and *asteroids* that orbit our Sun. Initially, the planetesimals hurtled through space until they crashed into one another. When they collided, they sometimes shattered into a billion pieces. But sometimes they stuck together, forming a larger object.

Eventually a few large objects formed. Close to the Sun, four small terrestrial, or Earth-like, planets with rocky surfaces formed. The lighter gases on Mercury, Venus, Earth, and Mars were heated by the Sun and quickly evaporated. Farther away, material condensed into gas giants.

Saturn is the sixth planet from the Sun. On average, its orbit is more than 888 million miles (1.4 billion kilometers) from the Sun,

Saturn and Earth

Vital Statistics

	Saturn	Earth
AVERAGE DISTANCE FROM THE SUN	888,187,993 miles (1,429,400,000 kilometers)	92,955,808 miles (149,597,870 km)
DIAMETER AT THE EQUATOR	74,900 miles (120,540 km)	7,926 miles (12,756 km)
MASS	95.18	1.00
VOLUME	744	1.00
DENSITY	0.69	5.52
SURFACE TEMPERATURE	−292 degrees Fahrenheit (−180 degrees Celsius)	−94 to 130°F (−70 to 54.4°C)
PERIOD OF REVOLUTION (LENGTH OF ONE YEAR)	29.46 Earth-years	365.24 Earth-days
PERIOD OF ROTATION (LENGTH OF ONE DAY)	10.54 hours	23.93 hours
NAMED MOONS	18*	1

* As many as twelve additional moons have been sighted, but they do not yet have official names.

and it takes nearly 30 Earth-years to complete one *revolution*. The queen of the planets is more than 9.5 times farther from the Sun than Earth and nearly twice as far from the Sun as Jupiter. Saturn is so far away from the Sun that solar rays did not evaporate the hydrogen and helium in its atmosphere. Even today, these gases are the main ingredients that make up Saturn.

Watching a Distant Jewel

In ancient times, skywatchers saw the planet Saturn as a faint, steadily glowing object in the night sky. Early observers recorded Saturn's movements and tracked the changes they could see. For many cultures, Saturn represented a character in mythology, and the planet had many names.

The Sumerians named the planet Ubu-idim or Sag-us, and the ancient Chinese called it Tu xing. The Babylonians called the planet Ninib or Nin-urta, meaning "the star belonging to the god Genna," and made careful records of its movements. The Mesopotamians noticed that Saturn moves more slowly than any other planet they could see—taking almost 30 years to make a complete tour across the star constellations in the sky.

In Hindu mythology, the planet Saturn is connected with the god Sani, who is known as "the evil-eyed one." One powerful look from Sani's dreadful eyes could cause anything to burst into flame instantly. Sani's parents were the Sun god Surya and the goddess Chaya, whose name means "shadow." The Hindus believed that Saturn and the other planets formed a planetary council.

For ancient Greeks, Saturn was the "star of Kronos," whose son Zeus became the king of the gods. The Greeks thought of Saturn as a sort of fallen king, displaced by the Sun, and they called the planet the "sun of the night."

In Roman mythology, Kronos was called Saturn, and that's the name we use to describe the planet today. Each year, the ancient Romans honored the god Saturn—the god of planting and harvest—and his wife Ops—the goddess of plenty—with an extravagant

According to some historians, the Roman god Saturn inspired festivities similar to our Christmas traditions of exchanging gifts and inviting family members to feasts.

weeklong celebration called Saturnalia. Some historians believe that many of our modern Christmas customs and rituals have their roots in the Roman Saturnalia.

The Planet with "Handles"

In the early 1600s, European sailors began using a new invention—the telescope—to search for distant shores. As soon as Italian astronomer Galileo Galilei heard about the telescope, he envisioned a different use for this incredible new instrument. He wanted to view all the glorious details of the Moon, the planets, and the stars.

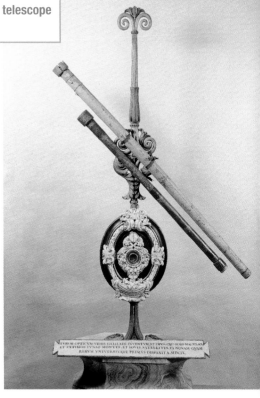

In 1610, Galileo built his own telescope and began to observe objects in space. When he pointed his telescope at Saturn, he saw something that surprised him. The planet appeared to have "handles" on each side of its yellow globe. At times, in fact, Saturn seemed to be a "triple" planet. Galileo told others, "I have observed the highest planet [Saturn] to be triple-bodied. This is to say that to my very great amazement Saturn was seen to me to be not a single star, but three together, which almost touch each other."

Galileo continued his studies of Saturn for many years, but he was never able to fully explain the planet's unusual appearance. Before scientists could understand Saturn, they needed to develop more powerful telescopes.

Using a larger, better telescope, the Dutch physicist and astronomer Christiaan Huygens finally solved the "handle" mystery. At first, Huygens wrote about his amazing discovery in code. He wanted to establish proof that he was the first person to notice Saturn's rings, but he didn't want to make a public announcement until he double-checked his observations. In 1659, when Huygens was sure

The Dutch astronomer Christiaan Huygens saw that Saturn's "handles" were actually a ring, completely separate from the planet.

that what he had seen was real, he decoded his announcement. It declared that Saturn is surrounded by "a thin, flat ring, nowhere touching . . ." the planet.

Cassini: A Keen Observer

Giovanni Domenico Cassini (1625–1712) was born and educated in Italy. He first explored *astronomy*—the scientific study of the universe—to disprove *astrology*—the belief that human lives are governed by the alignment of stars and planets at the time of a person's birth.

In 1669, Louis XIV, king of France, invited Cassini to move to the Paris Observatory. The astronomer remained there for the rest of his life. He became a French citizen and is often referred to by the French version of his name— Jean Dominique Cassini. In Paris, he used telescopes more than 100 feet (30 m) long to discover the moons Iapetus, Rhea, Dione, and Tethys.

Cassini competed fiercely with Dutch astronomer Christiaan Huygens and was happy to one-up Huygens by announcing that Saturn's "ring" was actually two rings divided by a wide gap. Cassini also suggested that the rings were composed of many separate particles.

Giovanni Domenico Cassini was a French-Italian astronomer who discovered four of Saturn's moons and a wide gap in its rings, now called Cassini's Division in his honor.

In 1675, Italian-born astronomer Giovanni Domenico Cassini was observing the ring Huygens had discovered 20 years earlier. He noticed a dark band within the ring and realized that it must be a gap between two separate rings. Saturn had two rings—not one! To honor Cassini, the gap was named Cassini's Division.

Today we know that Saturn is surrounded by at least seven rings. Most of the particles that make up these rings are very small, ranging from the size of a marble to the size of a basketball.

Satellite Search

Even before realizing what Saturn's "handles" really were, Huygens made another exciting discovery—Saturn's largest moon, Titan. He found the new *satellite* in 1655 using a telescope he had designed himself. With a diameter of 3,200 miles (5,150 km), Titan is the second-largest moon in the solar system—even larger than the planets Mercury and Pluto. Unlike Jupiter's large moons, Titan is the only large moon orbiting Saturn. It is three to five times bigger than Saturn's other moons.

By the end of the seventeenth century, Cassini had found four more moons around Saturn. He spotted Iapetus in 1671, Rhea in 1672, and Tethys and Dione in 1684. All four are medium-sized, highly reflective bodies that travel in orbits outside the planet's rings.

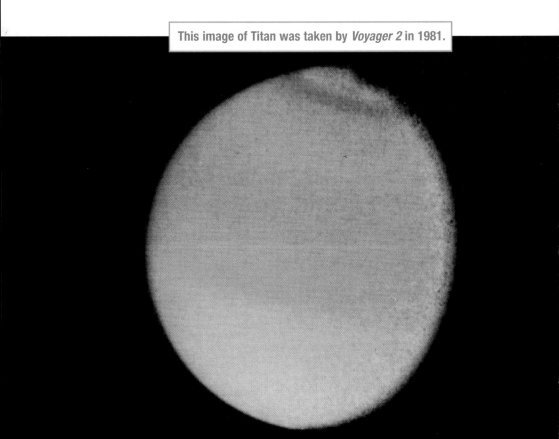

This image of Titan was taken by *Voyager 2* in 1981.

Chapter 2

Grand Voyages

Saturn's rings and moons piqued scientists' curiosity about the planet. They wondered what other secrets the queen of the planets had in store for us. Over the next 200 years, scientists spotted several more moons and made other intriguing discoveries, but the most exciting information about Saturn—and the first close-up views—came in the late 1900s.

By the 1970s and early 1980s, the U.S. National Aeronautics and Space Administration (NASA) had established a strong working relationship with the California Institute of Technology's Jet Propulsion Laboratory (JPL). During these two decades, JPL developed and managed four exciting NASA missions to explore the gas giants. Three of the missions included visits to Saturn.

The Jet Propulsion Laboratory in Pasadena, California, manages many of NASA's missions to the planets.

The first mission, *Pioneer 10*, was launched on March 2, 1972. The spacecraft sped straight for Jupiter, flew by, and snapped the first close-up images of that mighty planet. Then, without visiting Saturn, it headed toward the edge of the solar system. The next spacecraft, *Pioneer 11*, became the first visitor to Saturn. It was launched on April 5, 1973. Like *Pioneer 10*, it flew by Jupiter first. Then *Pioneer 11* used a nudge from Jupiter's *gravitational field* to accelerate and swing by the ringed planet.

Several years later, NASA launched two more sophisticated spacecraft—the Voyagers. *Voyager 1* arrived at Saturn in 1980, and *Voyager 2* followed in 1981. Compared to the *Pioneer 11* pictures, the images from the Voyagers were breathtaking. The difference might be compared to a comic book drawing versus a full-color, high-resolution photograph. Even today, scientists continue to study and learn new things from the thousands of images returned by these hardy spacecraft.

Pioneer 11 Takes a Peek

On September 1, 1979, *Pioneer 11* became the first spacecraft to visit Saturn. It flew within 2,175 miles (3,500 km) of Saturn's outermost ring—the A ring. Then *Pioneer 11* dipped below the rings and sailed

Pioneer 11 may have looked like this as it approached Saturn.

about 13,005 miles (20,930 km) above Saturn's cloud tops. The spacecraft confirmed the existence of the planet's E ring and discovered a new ring, which scientists now call the F ring. It also discovered several new moons and measured those that were already familiar, including Saturn's largest moon—Titan.

Equipment on board *Pioneer 11* also took measurements to help scientists learn about Saturn's inner layers. The data indicated that Saturn has a rocky inner core that probably has about the same diameter as Earth, but is much denser. Based on this information, researchers estimate that Saturn's core is three times more massive than our entire planet.

Voyager Visits

Voyager 2 was launched on August 20, 1977. *Voyager 1* was launched a few weeks later, on September 5, 1977, but it arrived at Saturn first. How did that happen? It was all part of NASA's intricate master plan. *Voyager 1* flew straight to Jupiter, then to Saturn so it could take a close look at Saturn's mysterious moon Titan. Finally, it headed for the edge of the solar system.

Voyager 2 was launched earlier, but headed toward the Sun. It swung around Venus and then passed Earth, picking up momentum from the gravitational fields of both planets. NASA had planned this flight to coincide with an unusual planetary alignment that occurs only once every 189 years. As a result, *Voyager 2* was able to fly by all four of the outer solar system's gas giants.

The two spacecraft, *Voyager 1* and *Voyager 2,* added immensely to scientists' knowledge of Jupiter, Saturn, Uranus, and Neptune, their moons, and their rings. Many of the biggest surprises came when the two Voyagers reached Saturn. The twin Voyager spacecraft found that the weather on Saturn is relatively calm compared with that on Jupiter. They detected massive jet streams that move relatively slowly and vary slightly from one another. The Voyagers also confirmed *Pioneer 11*'s observations that Saturn is a giant ball of gases, and has a composition very similar to Jupiter's.

This illustration shows an artist's view of *Voyager 2*'s exciting arrival at Saturn, silhouetted against the huge planet and its rings.

Science at Work: Getting a Boost

There is a limit to how much fuel a spacecraft can carry into space from a rocket launch. For every drop of fuel added to power the launch rocket, more fuel is needed to carry the additional weight. So in the early days of planetary exploration, NASA engineers came up with a clever idea for going farther on less fuel and packing more missions into one spaceflight. They could use the gravitational force of the planets to boost a spacecraft as it passes by. This technique, known as a *gravity assist*, has the added advantage of allowing a spacecraft to visit other planets and do additional research on the way to its main destination.

Using this boost, *Voyager 2* was able to "slingshot" from planet to planet, making important and exciting observations all along the way. As one scientist put it, "Every Voyager image that came in had something new." As the spacecraft approached each planet, it swung past in an arc, gaining momentum and speed for the next leg of the journey. Later, NASA used this technique over and over.

The spacecraft also spotted seven previously unknown moons and discovered several surprises as they skimmed by some of Saturn's known moons. Voyager images showed that Mimas, first spotted in 1789 by British astronomer William Herschel, has a huge impact crater that makes the moon look like a giant eyeball. Although Tethys, one of Saturn's larger moons, was discovered in the late 1600s by Cassini, it was Voyager that showed scientists the moon's most extraordinary feature—a huge canyon, or trench, that stretches most of the way around the moon's circumference.

In addition, the Voyager visit to Titan revealed that the big moon has a smoggy, murky atmosphere rather than white, fluffy, Earth-like clouds. Despite this difference, Titan has a great deal in common with a primitive planet. Researchers hope that further exploration of Titan may provide clues about how Earth's chemistry has changed over time and why life evolved on our planet.

Mimas's big crater makes it look like a giant eyeball.

Even bigger surprises were in store for scientists intrigued by Saturn's rings. The Voyagers revealed that the rings of Saturn are far more complex than anyone had imagined. They are a nonstop swirling mixture of dust particles, tiny ice crystals, hailstones, snowballs, and huge rounded blocks of ice. The rings feature intricate arrangements that include kinked ringlets, thin braided strands, spokes, and

Saturn's rings are made up of a jumble of large and small particles, as shown in this illustration.

scalloped edges. The Voyager spacecraft also showed scientists that Saturn is not the only planet in the solar system with rings. Jupiter, Uranus, and Neptune have them too.

Twenty-First-Century Visit

The two Voyager spacecraft made an amazing tour of the Saturn system, packed with new views and stunning vistas. Scientists received enormous quantities of new information. Along with *Pioneer 11*, *Voyager 1* and *Voyager 2* transformed our view of the queen of the planets. For thousands of years, people thought of Saturn as a tiny, faraway, top-like toy, but after these missions people began to view Saturn as a giant, commanding world with an amazing retinue of moons and rings.

Scientists were so fascinated by Saturn and its family that they wanted to send another spacecraft to collect even more data. So NASA

The Cassini-Huygens mission lifted off
from Cape Canaveral, Florida, in 1997.

teamed up with the European Space Agency (ESA) to plan the Cassini-
Huygens mission, which is named after the pioneering astronomers
Giovanni Domenico Cassini and Christiaan Huygens.

The Cassini-Huygens spacecraft was launched on October 15,
1997, but it will not reach Saturn until 2004. Because Saturn is so far
away, even the powerful rocket that launched *Cassini-Huygens* could
not propel the spacecraft directly to the queen of the planets. But

After Linda Spilker graduated from college in 1977, she began working for NASA's Jet Propulsion Laboratory in Pasadena, California. For Spilker, the job was the beginning of an exciting career exploring planets. For the next 13 years, she worked with the Voyager Infrared Team as the Voyager mission visited Jupiter, Saturn, Uranus, and Neptune. "Voyager's discoveries were astounding!" she recalls.

Spilker was fascinated by Saturn's rings and wanted to spend more time studying them, but she knew she would need to complete more studies first. So she decided to go back to school and, in 1992, earned a Ph.D. in geophysics and space physics from the University of California, Los Angeles.

Today, Spilker is the Cassini Deputy Project Scientist and a member of the Cassini Composite Infrared Team. Her biggest challenge is to make sure that *Cassini*'s visit to Saturn includes as many productive science experiments as possible. She spends a large part of her time talking with other scientists about what they would like to see *Cassini* accomplish.

As a researcher, Spilker also continues to work with data from the Voyager missions. She runs computer models and explores the complex workings of Saturn's rings. Spilker says she is always learning new things about them. This is important because the more she knows about the rings, the more effectively she will oversee *Cassini*'s work.

Linda Spilker, an expert in space physics, is Deputy Project Scientist for the Cassini mission.

mission planners knew they could use a series of gravity assists to thrust the spacecraft into the outer solar system.

During its flight, *Cassini-Huygens* has taken advantage of the gravitational fields of three planets. It looped around Venus twice, swung past Earth, and headed for Jupiter, arriving there in December 1999. Then the spacecraft whipped past Jupiter to slingshot on toward Saturn.

Scientists hope that *Cassini-Huygens* will answer some of the questions raised by the Voyager missions. When the two-part spacecraft finally arrives in Saturn's neighborhood, it will slow down and enter orbit around the giant planet. After it has made one complete revolution around the planet, the spacecraft's two parts will separate. *Cassini* will continue to orbit Saturn for at least 4 years and carry out close-up studies of as many of Saturn's moons as possible.

Meanwhile, the *Huygens* probe will plunge into Titan's atmosphere. The probe has three parachutes and a heat shield to protect its aluminum body as it falls toward the moon's surface and then gently touches down. If everything goes according to plan, the probe will take more than 1,000 photographs of Titan's surface and transmit them to the Cassini orbiter, which will then send the images to scientists on Earth.

Chapter 3

The Golden Globe

Like the clouds around Jupiter, the clouds in Saturn's upper atmosphere form bands. Jupiter's colorful red, orange, brown, and white bands are easy to see, but Saturn's pale white, gray, and golden-butterscotch bands are less distinct. These multicolored stripes are evidence of forces at work inside and outside the planet.

Saturn rotates so rapidly that its atmosphere bulges out at the equator, giving the planet a pronounced oval shape. A day on the queen of the planets is just 10.54 hours long—the second-shortest in the solar system. The planet's rapid rotation causes the substances within its atmosphere to separate into colorful bands that run parallel to the planet's equator. Some bands contain very dense materials, while others contain materials with lower *densities*.

Voyager 2 took this stunning image of the queen of the planets in 1981.

Scientists believe that Saturn's subtle colors are the result of interactions between trace elements, such as sulfur and carbon compounds, and lightning or charged particles in the planet's upper atmosphere. Researchers have also noticed that Saturn's colors are most vivid where the Sun's heat is most intense—near the planet's equator.

Weather on Saturn

When scientists looked closely at images taken by the Voyager spacecraft, they noticed a variety of unusual spots, waves, and eddies in Saturn's atmosphere. These features were clear evidence that massive jet streams blow both east and west within Saturn's colorful cloud bands. However, detecting other weather patterns proved a bit more challenging.

Scientists were disappointed by images from *Voyager 1*. They quickly realized that if they wanted to track weather patterns within Saturn's atmosphere, they would have to photograph the planet more

This close-up of Saturn's clouds, taken by *Voyager 1*, shows their varied and complex structure.

frequently. So by the time *Voyager 2* arrived a few months later, they had made some adjustments to the spacecraft's imaging equipment.

As a result, when *Voyager 2* captured close-up images of Saturn's northern hemisphere, there was clear evidence of weather patterns that no one had ever seen before. The images revealed storm clouds and circular storm systems. Like thunderstorms and hurricanes on Earth, most of Saturn's storms are unpredictable and relatively short-lived.

The most notable exception is Saturn's Great White Spot—a very large storm that develops in Saturn's relatively calm atmosphere once every 29 or 30 years. Astronomers first noticed the Great White Spot

In this image, *Hubble Space Telescope* captured a rare view of a Saturn's Great White Spot—the triangle-shaped area just above the rings.

This computer-enhanced infrared image from *Hubble Space Telescope* shows the Great White Spot spreading to become stripe-shaped.

in 1876. It was also observed in 1903, 1933, 1960, and 1990. The timing of this storm is remarkably similar to the length of Saturn's year, which is 29.46 Earth-years long. As a result, astronomers think that this recurring storm may mark the end of summer on Saturn.

As summer heat warms up the planet's atmosphere, ammonia bubbles up and crystallizes. Winds up to 1,000 miles (1,609 km) per hour whip these crystals around the planet. In 1990, the Great White Spot started out with a diameter of 15,000 miles (24,140 km) and could be seen through backyard telescopes as a luminescent, bright light. The spot was visible for about a month and then spread out to form a thick white stripe that encircled the planet. This phase of the storm was photographed by the *Hubble Space Telescope.*

Inside Saturn

At the top of Saturn's atmosphere, the temperature is cold, ranging from −311.8 to −202°F (−191 to −130°C). Most *planetologists* think Saturn's colorful upper-cloud layer is a relatively thin cover that floats above an extensive, clear hydrogen-helium atmosphere. They also think that in the planet's lower atmosphere, the ratio of helium to hydrogen increases, the temperature steadily climbs, and the pressure keeps building.

At some point, the tremendous pressure of the gases above transforms the hydrogen and helium mixture into a vast, liquid ocean.

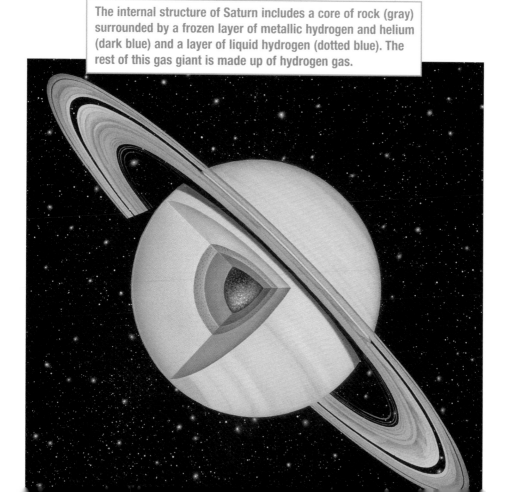

The internal structure of Saturn includes a core of rock (gray) surrounded by a frozen layer of metallic hydrogen and helium (dark blue) and a layer of liquid hydrogen (dotted blue). The rest of this gas giant is made up of hydrogen gas.

Moving even farther into the interior, the pressure becomes even greater. The crush of layer upon layer of gas finally destroys the hydrogen atoms and strips them of their electrons. As a result, the hydrogen becomes a metallic liquid that can conduct an electrical current.

The metallic hydrogen swirls as the planet rotates, creating Saturn's *magnetic field*. Like Earth and Jupiter, Saturn behaves like a giant bar magnet with north and south poles. While strong, the structure of Saturn's magnetic field is simple. It is symmetrical on all sides of the planet's axis.

Saturn also has a vast, invisible electromagnetic region called a *magnetosphere* that extends more than 3.9 million miles (6.4 million km) toward the Sun. Saturn's magnetosphere traps particles from *radiation belts* that surround the planet. These belts are bounded by the inner edges of the rings surrounding Saturn. The planet's rings and moons absorb any particles that collide with the radiation belts.

Saturn's magnetosphere may also spread outward toward the edge of the solar system in a long, broad tail of particles that are scattered by the *solar wind*—a stream of highly magnetic particles that flows at high speeds from the Sun's surface. Observations by the *Hubble Space Telescope* and other instruments have shown that Saturn's magnetosphere changes size and shape as it interacts with the solar wind.

Light Shows on Saturn

On October 9, 1994, the *Hubble Space Telescope* captured an image of an *aurora* on Saturn. Saturn's aurorae rise, like huge curtains of light, up to 1,200 miles (1,931 km) above the planet's cloud tops. They shimmer with rapidly changing brightness for several hours.

In this *Hubble Space Telescope image*, Saturn's aurorae appear as bright areas near the planet's poles.

As on Earth, aurorae on Saturn occur when charged particles from the planet's magnetosphere collide with particles in the solar wind. The bombardment causes Saturn's gases to glow with *ultraviolet radiation*. Unfortunately, the incredible light shows on Saturn cannot be seen by viewers on Earth because our planet's atmosphere absorbs ultraviolet radiation. However, *Hubble*, orbiting high above Earth's atmosphere, can catch the sensational displays and photograph them.

The first images of Saturn's aurorae were taken by *Pioneer 11* in 1979, when the spacecraft observed an ultraviolet brightening at the planet's poles. Then the *International Ultraviolet Explorer*, a spacecraft sponsored by several nations, observed a similar display in 1980. In 1997, *Hubble* was able to obtain even higher-resolution images. These photos revealed an aurora that consisted of a series of bright ripples and slowly evolving patterns.

Chapter 4

Rings, Ringlets, and Inner Moons

Ever since Galileo Galilei and Christiaan Huygens first spotted Saturn's rings in the seventeenth century, these stunning jewels have become Saturn's distinguishing feature for most people. Even though all four gas giants have rings, Saturn's rings are by far the most extraordinary and the most complex.

Through a backyard telescope, the rings of Saturn look something like a great golden speedway, with lanes marked but no cars. The "lane markings" are actually gaps between rings. Using high-power Earth-based telescopes, scientists can discern three separate rings and two gaps swirling around Saturn.

The A ring is the outermost ring visible from Earth. At least two moons—Pan and Atlas—orbit inside its boundaries. The A ring is split by the Encke Division, a narrow gap discovered in 1837 by a German astronomer named Johann Encke.

A broad gap separates the A ring from the B ring. As you learned earlier, this wide space was first noticed in 1675 by Cassini and is named the Cassini Division in his honor. Initially, the Cassini Division seemed empty to astronomers viewing it from Earth, but the Voyager spacecraft showed that thousands of tiny ringlets orbit there.

Cassini's Division—a big gap between Saturn's A ring and B ring—appears clearly in this computer-enhanced photo taken by *Voyager 1*.

This image clearly shows the "spoke" features in Saturn's B ring.

The B ring is wide and brighter than the A ring. Its material is also very tightly packed compared to material in Saturn's other rings. The B ring has a puzzling series of lines that seem to point outward like dark rays or spokes on a wheel. These strange markings are sometimes up to 12,427 miles (20,000 km) long—about the diameter of Earth. The Voyager spacecraft showed that these spokes seem to hover both above and below the rings. They also rotate at the same rate as the planet's magnetic field, so they may be clouds of dust particles caught in suspended patterns by Saturn's magnetic field.

The C ring is the faintest and the innermost ring visible from Earth. It was first noticed in 1850. For more than 100 years, astronomers believed that the C ring was Saturn's innermost ring, but images from *Voyager 1* proved them wrong. The spacecraft spotted several sparse, dusty, narrow bands between the C ring and Saturn's cloud tops. This region, which is practically impossible to observe from Earth, is now known as the D ring.

Voyager 1 was not the only spacecraft to change the way scientists think about Saturn's ring system. In 1979, *Pioneer 11* had shown scientists that the A ring is not Saturn's outermost ring. The spacecraft discovered another, smaller ring just 2,485 miles (4,000 km) beyond the A ring's outer edge. The F ring, as it is called, is bright but slender. Pioneer 11 images revealed a strange structure within this ring. In some places, the particles seem to weave over and under one another as if they had been braided by giant hands.

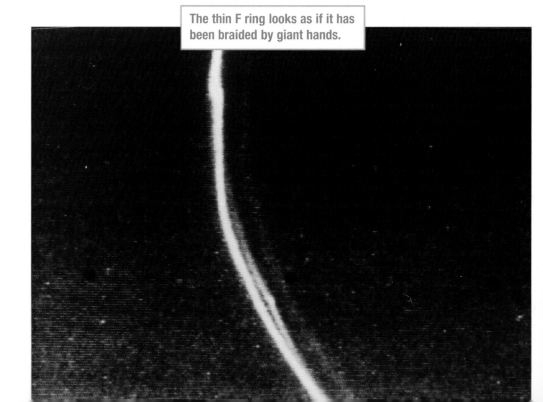

The thin F ring looks as if it has been braided by giant hands.

Saturn's Ring System

Vital Statistics

Feature	Distance from Saturn's Center	Description
D Ring	37,282 miles (60,000 km)	A very faint ring located just above Saturn's cloud tops, discovered by *Pioneer 11*
Guerin Division	45,112 miles (72,600 km)	A 746-mile (1,200-km)-wide gap between the D and C rings
C Ring	45,857 miles (73,800 km)	One of the first three rings to be discovered
Maxwell Division	57,042 miles (91,800 km)	A tiny, 311-mile (500-km)-wide gap between the C and B rings
B Ring	57,353 miles (92,300 km)	Second ring discovered; nearly 16,000 miles (26,000 km) wide
Cassini Division	71,955 miles (115,800 km)	A 2,983-mile (4,800-km)-wide gap between the B and A rings
A Ring	74,937 miles (120,600 km)	First ring discovered; nearly 10,000 miles (16,000 km) wide
Encke Division	82,394 miles (132,600 km)	A split within the A ring; discovered in 1837 by German astronomer Johann Encke
F Ring	87,400 miles (140,600 km)	A narrow ring, only 62 miles (100 km) wide, composed of 3 partly "braided" strands
G Ring	93,206 miles (115,000 km)	An extremely faint ring
E Ring	149,129 miles (240,000 km)	A wide, diffuse ring that encompasses the orbit of Enceladus

Eventually, scientists also discovered the E ring—a very faint, sparse scattering of particles in the same plane as the other rings and Saturn's moons. It is composed of tiny particles of dust and extends all the way out to the orbit of the moon Rhea. The orbit of the satellite Enceladus is located within the E ring, and some scientists think that this little moon may be the source of the E ring's material. Saturn's seventh ring—the G ring—is even sparser than the E ring, and it is very narrow—only 4,971 miles (8,000 km) wide.

The Tilted View

Two years after Galileo first observed Saturn's "handles," he noticed something even more unbelievable. First the handles vanished, and then they reappeared. Galileo was baffled by these observations. He couldn't come up with any explanation for what he saw.

Today, scientists know that Galileo was the first person to observe an optical trick called a "ring plane crossing." During times when Saturn's "handles" seem to mysteriously disappear, Earth's orbit is directly in line with the plane of Saturn's rings. As a result, observers on Earth are looking at the rings edge-on.

Saturn's rings are very thin—about as thick as the height of a 10-story building in some places! That's why they seem to disappear when the relative positions of Earth and Saturn place the rings in an edge-on view. No wonder Galileo was confused!

Saturn is tipped on its axis differently from Earth. So at different points in its orbit around the Sun, Saturn seems to tilt in different directions. Sometimes, the rings are on edge, and they look like a thin line cutting across the middle of the planet. When Saturn's northern hemisphere is tipped toward the Sun, viewers on Earth can see the top, or northern, side of the rings. When Saturn turns its southern hemisphere toward the Sun, the bottom, or southern, side of the rings becomes visible. For viewers on Earth, these changes can make Saturn look dramatically different at various points in its orbit.

When scientists became aware of Saturn's rings and of the relative positions of Earth's orbit and Saturn's tilt and orbit, they realized the advantage this situation could have for observing other objects in Saturn's neighborhood. Without the glare and brightness from the reflected Sun on the rings, it was easier to spot Saturn's moons—especially those closest to the planet.

When Saturn's rings are seen on-edge from Earth, as they are in this photo, some of Saturn's moons are easier to see.

However, seen from Voyager's viewpoint, the rings always look like a very broad speedway. From the outer edge to the inner edge, including gaps, they are 169,000 miles (272,000 km) wide.

Where Did the Rings Come From?

In the 1800s, a French mathematician named Edward (1820–1883) predicted that if a moon gets too close to a p' planet's gravity will cause the moon to disintegrate. A Roche's calculations, if a planet and moon have the same catastrophe will take place if the moon is closer to the planet than 2.44 times the planet's *radius*. This distance is now known as Roche's limit.

The rings of all four gas giant planets, including Saturn, are within Roche's limit. As a result, many scientists think the rings of all four planets may be the leftovers of disintegrated moons. Of course, this calculation does not take other factors into account. For example, the type of material a moon is made of and its ability to stick together could keep a moon from breaking up, even within Roche's limit—and that could explain why Saturn's rings contain several small moons.

Saturn is not the only planet with rings. This artist's view of *Voyager 2* flying by Uranus in 1986 shows some of the blue-green planet's eleven rings.

In the 1960s, scientists began using an instrument known as a *spectroscope* to study Saturn's rings. From their experiments, we now know that Saturn's rings contain—or are at least coated with—water ice. In fact, Saturn's golden shimmer comes mostly from the bright reflections of sunlight bouncing off the planet's icy rings.

Some spectacular Voyager images of Saturn's rings have been colorized to show all the different materials found in the ring particles. These images seem to show that the three big rings each have trace elements of different origins. One Voyager scientist, the late Eugene Shoemaker, concluded that three different parent bodies may have fragmented to form the A, B, and C rings.

Another theory suggests that the material in the rings has existed there since the formation of the solar system and is part of the material that surrounded Saturn as it formed. Advocates of this idea claim that since the rings fall within Roche's limit, the materials they are made of could not coalesce, or clump together, to form a moon. Over time, the materials became more and more scattered as particles collided and interacted.

The tiny moons that did form within this region may be so small compared to the mass of Saturn that they are not

Tiny satellites like this shepherd moon may be too small to be affected by Saturn's tidal forces.

affected by the planet's *tidal forces*—the difference between the force of gravity on the near and far sides of an object. For the same reason, astronauts returning to Earth are not torn apart by our planet's tidal forces. The tidal forces become insignificant on anything—or anyone—so small.

All the moons that move through and nearby Saturn's rings are dodging dangerously close to an enormous planet. At this distance, they are at great risk of bombardment by asteroids and other bodies attracted to the planet by its mass. As a result, some scientists have suggested that each of the rings may have started out as a moon that took a direct hit from a high-speed space rock. When each moon shattered, its fragments were trapped by Saturn's gravity and became an orbiting ring. While this theory is possible, many scientists discount it as much less likely than the other two ideas.

Why Doesn't Saturn Swallow Them Up?

According to mythology, Kronos—the Greek counterpart of Saturn—swallowed his children. It's an ancient story, with no real connection to the planet, yet an opportunity for comparison seems to exist. Saturn is a huge object with an enormous gravitational field, so why don't the particles that make up Saturn's rings "fall" into the planet? Why doesn't Saturn's giant gravitational field pull them in?

Scientists know that, once in orbit, particles tend to continue orbiting. However, in this case, that explanation does not seem to be sufficient. Most scientists believe that "shepherd moons," the little moons that orbit close to the edges of the rings, keep the particles in Saturn's rings stable and orbiting in an orderly fashion. Apparently, these moons organize, or shepherd, the smaller chunks of material.

Why don't the millions of pieces of ice in Saturn's rings "fall" into the planet? Shepherd moons make sure they don't stray.

When the Voyager spacecraft surveyed Saturn's rings, scientists discovered that the gravity of these shepherd moons combines with the gravity of larger neighboring moons to control the edges of the rings and keep the smaller particles from straying. Some scientists had predicted the existence of shepherd moons, so researchers were delighted when the Voyager spacecraft discovered them.

The shepherd moons also cause the smaller ring particles to bump into one another, which creates waves, wakes, and other interesting patterns in the rings. Researchers frequently use computers to create models of Saturn's rings to see how the various players influence one other.

Six named shepherd moons travel very close to the outer or inner edge of one of Saturn's rings. The first pair is Pan and Atlas—the two innermost named moons. They orbit within the A ring. Pan, the most

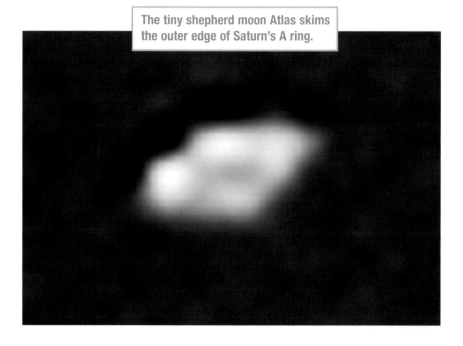

The tiny shepherd moon Atlas skims the outer edge of Saturn's A ring.

recently discovered of Saturn's officially named satellites, travels closer to Saturn than any other known moon. Its orbit falls within the Encke Division of the A ring. Scientists think Pan keeps order in this region.

Pan was first observed in 1990. Scientists spotted it in photos taken by *Voyager 2* a decade earlier. The moon's existence was predicted by studies of the Voyager photos. Atlas, discovered in 1980, orbits near the outer edge of the A ring. Like Pan, it is probably a shepherd satellite.

Pandora and Prometheus are two small moons that shepherd the F ring. Prometheus travels on the inner edge of the slender ring, and its partner, Pandora, orbits on the outer edge. Both of these small, irregularly shaped satellites were discovered by *Voyager 1* in 1980.

The craggy moon Pandora "shepherds" the F ring, as illustrated in this painting.

When astronomers observed Prometheus during a ring plane crossing in 1995 and 1996, they realized that the moon had unexpectedly slowed in its orbit. Perhaps the little moon was struck by debris and the force of the impact changed the moon's speed.

Around the same time, the *Hubble Space Telescope* discovered what may be an additional shepherding moon nearby. Tentatively known as S 1995 S/3 until its orbit is confirmed, some astronomers think the new moon may be responsible for the F ring's strange, braided appearance.

The next pair of shepherd moons, Epimetheus and Janus, share an orbit within the G ring—a sparsely populated ring of minute, nearly invisible material. As they move around Saturn, the moons play a strange, never-ending game of hopscotch. Each one takes a turn following the other. As the distance between the moons decreases, gravitational effects cause the moons to exchange orbits, so that the

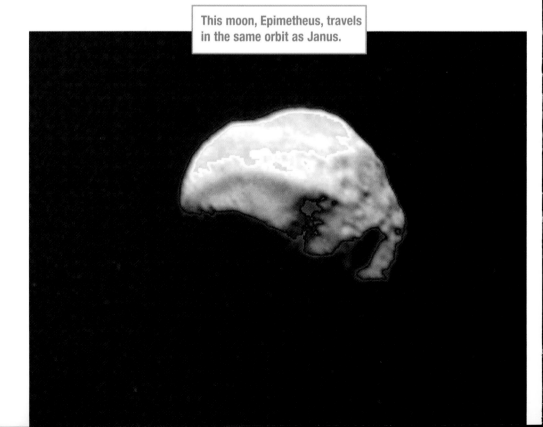

This moon, Epimetheus, travels in the same orbit as Janus.

leader suddenly becomes the follower. Then the game begins again, until the new follower reclaims its leading position at 4-year intervals.

These six shepherd moons are just the beginning of Saturn's big family of moons. The queen of the planets currently has eighteen named moons. Recently, astronomers have discovered as many as twelve more moons around Saturn. If all of these moons are eventually confirmed and named, Saturn will have a total of thirty satellites—more than any other planet in the solar system!

Chapter 5

Extended Family

Saturn is about 888,187,993 miles (1,429,400,000 km) away from the Sun. So far from the Sun's bright, warm rays, Saturn's neighborhood is a very cold place. No liquid water can exist here, but water ice is an important component of all Saturn's moons—with the exception of the planet's large, mysterious moon Titan.

As you know, Saturn's six inner moons—Pan, Atlas, Prometheus, Pandora, Epimetheus, and Janus—are very small and travel within the rings. The rest of the planet's satellites range from small—under 20 miles (32 km) on the long side—to nearly 1,000 miles (1,609 km) across. Some are pockmarked, jagged, and oddly shaped. Others are round and more like our own moon.

This illustration shows Saturn and the moons Mimas (closest to Saturn), Enceladus, Tethys, Dione, Rhea, Titan, and Hyperion (foreground).

Five of them—Mimas, Enceladus, Tethys, Telesto, and Calypso—orbit near the outer edges of the rings, and influence them. Another four—Dione, Helene, Rhea, and Titan—travel in intermediate orbits. Three—Hyperion, Iapetus, and Phoebe—are very distant and have highly *elliptical*, or flattened orbits that are inclined, or tipped at an angle. The four to six new, unnamed moons sighted in 2000 also belong to this group.

Bulging Eye

Of the six satellites beyond the A ring, Mimas travels closest to Saturn. Its orbit is located between the two faint outermost rings—the G and E rings. Some scientists suspect that Mimas may keep the Cassini Division, the big gap between the A and B rings, clear of particles.

Mimas is one of Saturn's spherical moons, but it is only 243 miles (392 km) in diameter. Thanks to a huge crater that extends across Mimas's face, the moon looks like a strange, bulging eyeball. This cavity, which dominates the moon's surface, is known as Herschel Crater. It has towering cliffs 32,800 feet (10,000 m) high. That's higher than Mount Everest—the tallest mountain on Earth.

The crater measures 80 miles (130 km) across—one-third of Mimas's diameter—and the peak formed at its center stands 13,123 feet (4,000 m) high. Scientists think the crater must have been caused by an enormous impact that nearly demolished this small world.

Some experts think Mimas may once have been part of a larger moon that was blown to pieces by a *meteoroid* or asteroid as it zoomed toward Saturn's cloud tops. This moon's heavily pocked surface shows that many space rocks have smashed into its surface. In fact, it has received twelve times more hits than Saturn's other outer moons.

Herschel Crater stretches across one-third of Mimas's surface.

Orbiting only 115,280 miles (185,520 km) from Saturn, Mimas has obviously been a prime target for a very long time. Nearby fragments seem to support this theory, and some scientists think the history of Mimas may be closely linked to the formation of the rings themselves.

Moon with a New Skin

Enceladus travels along the inside edge of the E ring. Of all the moons in Saturn's family, Enceladus has the youngest surface. It is also abnormally bright and shows the most geologic activity. Enceladus orbits 147,900 miles (238,020 km) from Saturn's center—about the distance of our Moon from Earth, but it is tiny by comparison. This moon measures only 311 miles (500 km) across, making it about half the size of Texas.

Like most of Saturn's moons, Enceladus is made mainly of water ice. However, its surface does not resemble any of Saturn's other moons. Mimas, Rhea, Dione, and Tethys are all heavily pitted. Their surfaces have not been smoothed or resurfaced for a very long time, but Enceladus has no scars or pockmarks. The little moon does have a few craters, but most of its surface is composed of broad, smooth plains.

Why is Enceladus so different from Saturn's other moons? What could have happened to it? Some process has intervened on this little moon, smoothing over the cracks and ridges and filling in the deep gouges and craters that must once have been there. Enceladus has had a facelift, but no one knows exactly how or why.

Two possibilities seem likely. The icy surface may have melted away and refrozen, or a flood may have poured over its surface and then frozen into a smooth, icy crust. Dark lines on the surface of the moon look like marks made with a felt pen. They are probably cracks

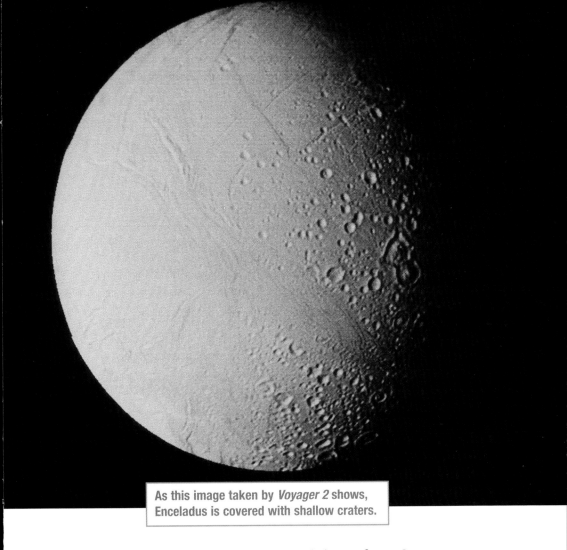

As this image taken by *Voyager 2* shows,
Enceladus is covered with shallow craters.

and fractures that formed in the crust and then refroze. Some recent source of heat must have caused this unusual flooding, followed by freezing, then cracking, and refreezing. Whatever happened, the strange event must have happened within the last several hundred million years. If more years had passed since the repaving, the moon's new skin would show a larger number of craters.

What caused the heating—especially when no other moons were affected? Scientists initially suspected that tidal forces were at work.

However, according to most calculations, Saturn's tidal forces are too weak to churn and heat the core of Enceladus. This is another one of the mysteries that future voyages to Saturn may help to solve.

"Our Kind" of Moons

Three moons orbiting beyond Enceladus seem like smaller versions of our own Moon. They are Tethys, Dione, and Rhea. Along with their more distant neighbor, Iapetus, these moons were discovered in the late seventeenth century by Giovanni Cassini. Although they are made of ice, their geology resembles the form we expected of moons before traveling spacecraft introduced us to the many different forms that moons can actually take.

Tethys, Dione, and Rhea are bright, spherical, and a little larger than most of Saturn's other moons—except Titan. Their surfaces are deeply pitted by layer upon layer of craters, many of which date back to the early formation of the solar system. Some regions display patches of darker tones that may be dirt. Streaks of bright, frosty material sweep across many of the cratered regions.

The innermost of these three moons, Tethys, revolves around Saturn only 36,000 miles (57,936 km) farther out than neighboring Enceladus. It orbits just beyond the outer edge of the sparse G ring. Tethys is only about one-third the size of Earth's Moon, and the Voyager spacecraft showed that its icy crust is marked with enormous cracks. One huge, gaping crack, the Ithaca Chasma, covers 75 percent of the moon's circumference. The crack is long enough to stretch from Boston, Massachusetts, to Los Angeles, California. Scientists speculate that the interior of Tethys was once liquid, covered with a crust that hardened rapidly. With every shift of the liquid interior, the hardened crust cracked and gaped.

This Voyager image shows Tethys (left) and
Dione as they orbit the queen of the planets.

This painting shows how Saturn might look if it were viewed across the cracked surface of Tethys.

Voyager photos revealed two much smaller moons—Telesto and Calypso—tagging along with Tethys in the same orbit. These moons are so small and irregular that no one even noticed them as Voyager swept by. However, in 1981, as researchers pored over the thousands of images taken by the spacecraft, they discovered these two small moons parading in front of and behind Tethys as they orbit the ringed planet.

Dione, which orbits about 50,500 miles (81,272 km) farther from Saturn, is nearly the same size as Tethys. Like its neighbor, Dione shares its orbit with a much smaller satellite, Helene. But unlike Tethys's companions, Helene was discovered in 1980 by two Earth-based astronomers.

Dione is considerably denser than most of Saturn's satellites, and scientists believe it may have a rocky core. Like our Moon, Dione

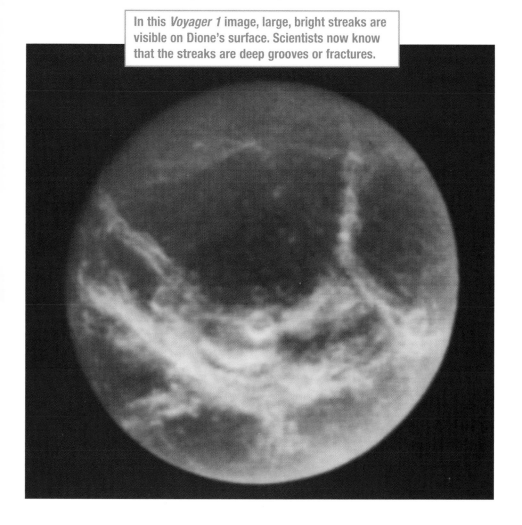

In this *Voyager 1* image, large, bright streaks are visible on Dione's surface. Scientists now know that the streaks are deep grooves or fractures.

always leads with the same hemisphere as it travels around the ringed planet. But, surprisingly, most of its craters are not on its leading edge. Why would more impacts occur on the side that is moving away from oncoming projectiles? Possibly, Dione has not always led with the same hemisphere. Some scientists speculate that a large impact may have spun the little moon around at some time in the recent past.

At 951 miles (1,530 km) in diameter, Rhea is larger than its nearby companions. It is about half the size of our Moon and seems to be a

Saturn's moon Rhea, shown in this image from *Voyager 1*, has a surface composed mostly of ice.

giant ball of frozen ice. It shows no signs of any geological activity, and ancient craters are piled on top of one another all over its surface. At about 327,500 miles (527,040 km) from Saturn, Rhea is about in the middle of Saturn's family.

The great moon Titan is more than twice as far from Saturn as Rhea, at a distance of 759,200 miles (1,221,780 km) from the planet. This enigmatic world is the only moon in the solar system that is veiled by a thick atmosphere, and its mysteries provide the subject of the next chapter.

Distant Outposts

The rest of Saturn's moons have orbits that average between almost 1 million and 8 million miles (1.6 and 12 million km) from the planet. These moons differ greatly from one another—and from Saturn's inner moons.

Hyperion is the largest irregularly shaped moon ever discovered. It is made of low-density, icy material and travels in a strangely flattened, highly *eccentric orbit.* Its heavily cratered surface displays deeply gouged pits and chasms. One of Hyperion's craters is 75 miles (120 km) across—more than 25 percent of the moon's diameter.

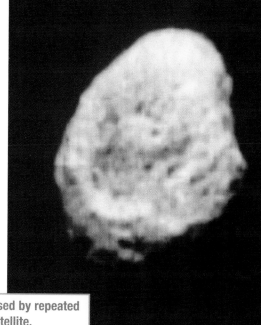

Hyperion's irregular shape was probably caused by repeated impacts that broke off large chunks of the satellite.

Planetologists have had difficulty explaining Hyperion's strange shape and unusual orbit. Perhaps a very large object hit the moon long ago, destroying part of the original moon and leaving behind this oddly shaped chunk of rock.

Iapetus is a spherical moon composed of ice and rock. Like Saturn's medium-sized "traditional" moons, Iapetus was discovered by Giovanni Cassini. Its leading edge—which is always the same—has a dark, reddish tinge, while its trailing side is bright white. No one is sure what the dark material is—possibly dust shed by Phoebe, the outermost of Saturn's moons. Another explanation could be that trapped deposits of methane, which are reddish in color, may have pushed out from the interior through cracks and crevices in the moon's

Voyager 2 captured this image of Iapetus in August 1981.

This painting shows Saturn between steep canyon walls on the surface of Phoebe.

crust, or it may be organic material similar to reddish hydrocarbons found on some ancient *meteorites* that have fallen to Earth. Like the other moons and rings of Saturn, scientists have much to learn about Iapetus and its intriguing history.

Unlike most of the other moons of Saturn, Iapetus travels in an orbit that is inclined to the plane of Saturn's rings. Viewed from Iapetus, Saturn's rings would be a truly spectacular sight. They would appear as a wide series of golden bands glimmering brightly with reflected sunlight against the dark background of a starry sky.

Phoebe, a small and lonely traveler, orbits at the far outer edge of Saturn's family. It moves in the opposite direction of the rest of Saturn's moons, in what is known as a *retrograde* orbit. As *Voyager 2* flew by

Named Moons of Saturn

Vital Statistics

Moon	Diameter*	Distance from Saturn's Center	Year of Discovery
PAN	12 miles (20 km)	83,015 miles (133,600 km)	1990
ATLAS	23.6 miles (38 km)	85,500 miles (137,600 km)	1980
PROMETHEUS	92 miles (148 km)	86,557 miles (139,300 km)	1980
PANDORA	68 miles (110 km)	88,048 miles (141,700 km)	1980
EPIMETHEUS	85.7 miles (138 km)	94,120 miles (151,472 km)	1980
JANUS	137 miles (220 km)	94,120 miles (151,472 km)	1966
MIMAS	243 miles (392 km)	115,280 miles (185,520 km)	1789
ENCELADUS	311 miles (500 km)	147,900 miles (238,020 km)	1789
TETHYS	653 miles (1,050 km)	183,000 miles (294,500 km)**	1684
TELESTO	18.6 miles (30 km)	183,000 miles (294,500 km)**	1981
CALYPSO	18.6 miles (30 km)	183,000 miles (294,500 km)**	1981
DIONE	696 miles (1,120 km)	234,500 miles (377,400 km)†	1684

Vital Statistics

Moon	Diameter*	Distance from Saturn's Center	Year of Discovery
HELENE	19.9 miles (32 km)	234,500 miles (377,400 km)†	1980
RHEA	951 miles (1,530 km)	327,500 miles (527,040 km)	1672
TITAN	3,200 miles (5,150 km)	759,200 miles (1,221,780 km)	1655
HYPERION	255 miles (410 km)	921,500 miles (1,483,000 km)	1848
IAPETUS	894 miles (1,440 km)	2,212,000 miles (3,560,000 km)	1671
PHOEBE	137 miles (220 km)	8,048,000 miles (12,952,000 km)	1898

* Many of Saturn's moons are irregularly shaped. In all cases, the diameter of the longest side is given.

** Tethys, Calypso, and Telesto share the same orbit.

† Dione and Helene share the same orbit.

Saturn it provided a brief look at Phoebe and recorded that this dark world is roughly spherical and about 137 miles (220 km) across. Phoebe's distance from Saturn, its retrograde orbit, and its dusky color all suggest that this moon was once an asteroid. As the little rock cruised through space, it may have been captured by Saturn's gravitational field.

All three of Saturn's farthest named outposts—Hyperion, Iapetus, and Phoebe—have a reddish tinge that may have come from Phoebe.

Since Phoebe is some 6 to 7 million miles (9.4 to 11.3 million km) away from the other two moons, this explanation may seem far-fetched. However, Phoebe's retrograde orbit may knock dust from the moon's surface into space and splatter it on both Hyperion and Iapetus.

How Many Moons?

When the Voyager spacecraft launched in 1977, Saturn had ten named moons, but that would soon change. In 1980 and 1981, *Voyager 1* caught sight of five previously unknown moons among the rings of Saturn, and *Voyager 2* spotted two new satellites sharing orbits with named moons. In just a few years, the number of known moons in Saturn's family had risen to seventeen. Then Pan was discovered from *Voyager 2* images years later, in 1990. These are the eighteen moons that are confirmed and named today.

During the 1995 ring plane crossing, the *Hubble Space Telescope* made seven new moon sightings, but most scientists think many of those objects may actually be different views of known moons. Until the orbits of the moons have been confirmed, they have been given tentative names, such as S 1995 S/1, which means "the first previously unknown satellite (S/1) of Saturn (the first S) reported in 1995." At least one of these moons, S 1995 S/3, was predicted by scientists. They believe it may be responsible for the strange, braided appearance of Saturn's F ring.

In 2000, an international team of astronomers discovered twelve more satellites in Saturn's family. These appear to be irregular moons like Phoebe, orbiting at least 9 million miles (14.4 million km) from

Saturn. Astronomers estimate that the new satellites are between 6 and 31 miles (10 and 50 km) across. Other astronomers at various observatories have made confirming observations, and most astronomers believe that at least four of these moons will eventually be confirmed by the International Astronomical Union and given names.

Chapter 6

Titan and the
Search for Life

Titan is the second-largest moon in the solar system. Only Jupiter's moon Ganymede is larger. With a diameter of 3,200 miles (5,150 km), Titan is one-third larger than Earth's Moon. At a distance of 759,200 miles (1,221,780 km) from Saturn's center, Titan orbits about three times farther away from its planet than our Moon orbits from Earth.

Titan is the only known moon with an atmosphere. This thick, hazy outer layer of gases along with the moon's rocky surface, make Titan more like Earth than any other object in the solar system. In addition, the molecules that exist within Titan's atmosphere and on its surface are the same as those present in Earth's early atmosphere.

This artwork shows what the surface of Titan may look like, with glimpses of Saturn seen through the clouds.

Exobiologists—scientists who study life, or conditions necessary for life, on other planets and moons—hope to learn more about how life may have developed and evolved on Earth by studying conditions on Titan.

Titan's atmosphere, like Earth's, is composed primarily of nitrogen. However, the other substances in Titan's atmosphere are different from those found on Earth today. There are most likely large quantities of such *hydrocarbons* as ethane and methane as well as traces of acetylene, propane, diacetylene, emethylacetylene, hydrogen cyanide, cyanoacetylene, cyanogen, carbon dioxide, and carbon monoxide. This atmosphere would certainly be poisonous to most of the creatures living on Earth today, but primitive life might thrive under such conditions.

Titan is very cold—a frigid –290°F (–178.9°C). Despite the incredible cold, it is possible that Titan has liquid oceans. While water freezes solid at 32°F (0°C), methane could exist as a gas, a liquid, or a frozen solid on Titan's surface. In fact, some scientists think that a source of liquid methane must exist on the surface of Titan to replenish the methane in the atmosphere. They claim that frozen methane would not release gas fast enough to form Titan's atmosphere.

According to one scientist, the liquid methane is probably mixed with ethane to produce a solution that is "mushy, gunky, and very dark." Scientists think Titan's smoggy haze forms when liquid methane rises from the ground, diffuses in the atmosphere, and is then destroyed by the Sun's ultraviolet radiation. The result is very similar to the smoggy air of Los Angeles, California.

In some places, the haze rises nearly 200 miles (320 km) above the big moon's surface. When the organic molecules stick together and become heavy, they would most likely fall back to the surface from the moon's atmosphere as very dirty rain.

Scientists who managed the development of the *Huygens* probe expect the small spacecraft to have a clear view of Titan from about 48 miles (80 km) above the surface. From that point down, researchers say, the haze clears and the visibility is good. On the way down, *Huygens* will spin, taking panoramic views of the surface as it twirls. Then it will touch down in a large bright area about the size of Australia. The spot was discovered by the *Hubble Space Telescope* in

In this futuristic painting, the *Huygens* probe speeds toward the surface of Titan. The probe's heat shield will prevent it from burning up in the big moon's atmosphere.

1994. No one is quite sure what the bright spot is. One theory suggests that the brightness may be caused by reflection off the high peaks of a methane-ice mountain range that is continually washed clean and eroded by methane rain.

During its thirty-five planned passes around Titan, the *Cassini* orbiter will use its onboard radar equipment to peer through the moon's thick clouds in search of liquid methane lakes or oceans. Other experiments on board the orbiter and probe will study the chemical processes that occur within Titan's thick atmosphere, including those that create the moon's unique haze.

Seeing the Surface

Peering through the dense atmosphere to get a peek at Titan's surface has always been a challenge. When Christiaan Huygens discovered Saturn's big moon in 1655, all he could see through his telescope was a blur. Although scientists have invented much more powerful telescopes since then, it is still difficult to view Titan from Earth.

Whenever scientists look at an object in space from an Earth-based telescope, they have to keep in mind that our planet's thick atmosphere is distorting the image. While it is not too difficult to compensate for the distortion caused by one atmosphere, astronomers viewing Titan must also compensate for the moon's atmosphere. In recent years, scientists have relied on sophisticated computer programs to determine how much an image is affected by each atmosphere and subtract that influence out of the final image.

Programming a computer to make all these adjustments is difficult and time consuming. That is why the first and some of the best images

Scientists would like to know why Titan's northern hemisphere is lighter in color than its southern hemisphere.

of Titan's surface features were captured by the *Hubble Space Telescope.* Because the orbiting telescope does not have to compensate for Earth's atmosphere, its camera equipment has a distinct advantage over cameras attached to telescopes on Earth

In recent years, scientists have begun to capture some good images of Titan's surface using infrared imaging techniques. In 2000, astronomer Athena Coustenis of the Paris-Meudon Observatory in France presented a series of images she obtained with the 142-inch (360-cm) Canada-France-Hawaii Telescope located in Hawaii. These

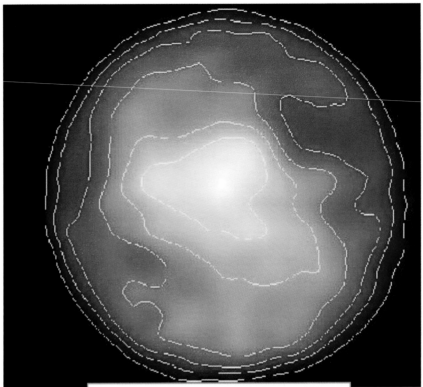

Athena Coustenis captured this image of Titan. Using a computer, she added the white lines to highlight areas with different brightnesses.

images show that a very bright, highly reflective area covers about 14 percent of the big moon's circumference.

Coustenis's images also show three brighter areas within the larger region of brightness. What are these bright areas? Coustenis and other scientists agree that an area of frozen methane could reflect in this way, especially if it extended high into the clouds. Perhaps the region consists of a high, mountainous plateau covered with ice. If so, these images suggest that the surface of Titan is covered with ice and rock.

While these results are encouraging, Coustenis and her colleagues admit that they were lucky to get such good images. At the time, viewing conditions were especially good. The telescope they were using was built atop a high mountain in a place with clear air. There, the obstructions of smog and city lights interfere less with visibility. In addition, their telescope had a new optical system that was especially good at compensating for blurring caused by the moving air of Earth's atmosphere.

Mapping Titan

The *Cassini* orbiter has onboard radar for mapping the surface of Titan. Using this equipment, scientists can detect geological features. Radar mapping works by sending out a microwave, or radar, signal from an instrument, bouncing it off a surface, and accurately recording the time it takes for the signal to return to the point of origin. When signals are sent in rapid succession, the results can be used to create a topographical map that shows the lay of the land—or the ocean.

Researchers can then use computers to convert the radar information into images that show what these features look like, much as if they were photographs. The images can be rotated to show peaks, cliffs, valleys, dips, folds, cracks, and crevices as they might look to a person standing on the big moon's surface. They can also identify liquid lakes or oceans. The radar images from *Cassini* could go a long way toward revealing what the mysterious surface of Titan is really like.

With this equipment, scientists expect to find out whether the surface of Titan is entirely solid or entirely liquid. Or, like Earth, Titan

An artist's interpretation of *Cassini* orbiting Titan.

may have landmasses dotted with lakes and surrounded by liquid oceans. Planetary scientist Don Miller thinks we could expect to find large bodies of liquid bound by craggy, rock-lined shores on Titan's surface. Among the rocks, he anticipates murky tide pools of dark-orange liquid reflecting the dense, gray-orange haze overhead. Another scientist suspects the moon's surface could be composed of a vast swampland, dotted with pools of liquid nitrogen and teeming with hydrocarbon goo. Both nitrogen and hydrocarbons were key ingredients for the origins of life on Earth.

Could There Be Life?

Cassini will also examine Titan's atmosphere and its makeup. No other satellite in our solar system has an atmosphere as abundant or complex as Titan's. Scientists would like to know exactly where the atmosphere came from and why the moon still retains such thick, gassy clouds. Could these clouds be composed of primordial gases that date back to the beginning of the big moon's creation? Were the gases trapped in the icy surface and released slowly over the ages? Could some very early precursors of microbial life possibly exist on Titan today?

What may happen to Titan in the future if its far-off, frigid climate becomes warmed by changes in the Sun? Right now, Titan's climate is much too cold for the formation of life as we know it. Yet, in many ways, the big moon is similar to early Earth. The moon has a primarily nitrogen atmosphere, a "chemistry lab" full of organic molecules, and the possible presence of both oceans and land.

In another 4 or 5 billion years, the temperature on Titan may become more inviting. By then, our Sun will have matured to become a *red giant*. The oceans of Earth will have boiled away. The Sun's heat will reach farther and farther out into the solar system. Eventually, its warmth will reach Titan, where it may encourage life to form and briefly evolve. Long after human life on Earth is gone, a new, though short, chapter of life in the solar system may begin on the moon that orbits the great ringed planet.

Chapter 7

More Mysteries to Solve

*V*oyagers *1* and *2* performed their jobs magnificently. They provided stunning views of the great ringed planet and insights about its astonishing rings and its varied family of satellites. They gave Earthbound scientists a new understanding of Saturn and its family.

The Voyagers' visits, though, were short, and scientists still have many questions about Saturn and its family. What internal processes occur deep in Saturn's interior and at its core? Is our current understanding of Saturn's atmospheric layers correct? How did the vast system of rings form, and why? What intriguing mysteries remain about their dynamics and their structure? Why doesn't the planet's gravitational field cause the rings to fall in toward their giant neighbor?

In 1980 and 1981, the Voyager spacecraft sent dozens of exciting photos of Saturn and reams information to this center at the Jet Propulsion Laboratory.

How does the influence of the shepherd moons work exactly? Does Titan have surface liquid in the form of ponds, lakes, or oceans? With its nitrogen atmosphere and its hydrocarbon-laden environment, can Titan offer any clues about the origins of life?

Perhaps the Cassini-Huygens mission will answer some of these questions. In the meantime, the search for answers goes on in other

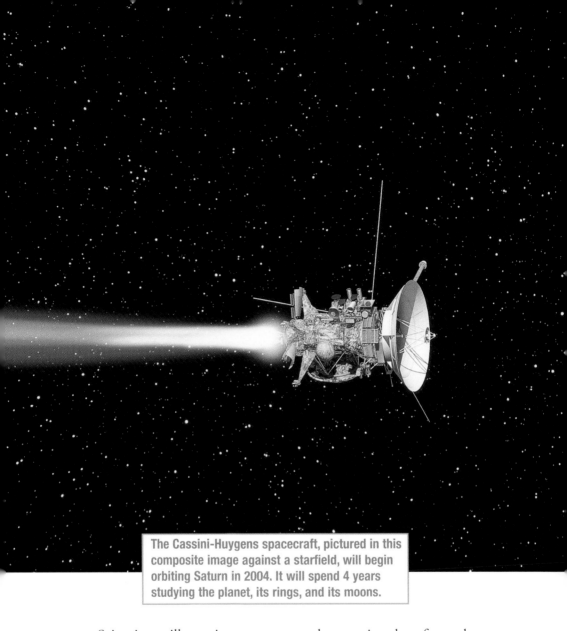

The Cassini-Huygens spacecraft, pictured in this composite image against a starfield, will begin orbiting Saturn in 2004. It will spend 4 years studying the planet, its rings, and its moons.

ways. Scientists will continue to survey the massive data from the Voyager visits, and they will find new ways to study the ringed planet and its large family.

Missions to Saturn

Vital Statistics

Spacecraft	Type of Mission	Year of Arrival	Sponsor
Pioneer 11	Flyby	1979	NASA
Voyager 1	Flyby	1980	NASA
Voyager 2	Flyby	1981	NASA
Cassini-Huygens	Orbiter and probe	2004	NASA/ESA

Exploring Saturn: A Timeline

1027 — Ancient Chinese observers note that Saturn briefly blocks Mars from view.

1610 — Galileo Galilei observes Saturn's rings, but does not understand what he is looking at.

1612 — Galileo notices that the rings of Saturn are not visible when seen side-on, but cannot explain his observations.

1655 — Christiaan Huygens discovers Saturn's largest moon, Titan, and proposes that Saturn is surrounded by a solid ring.

1659 — Huygens notices that every 14 to 15 years Earth passes through the plane of Saturn's rings, which makes them seem to disappear.

1671 — Giovanni Domenico Cassini discovers the moon Iapetus.

1672 — Cassini discovers the moon Rhea.

1675 — Cassini discovers a gap in the rings of Saturn, later called the Cassini Division.

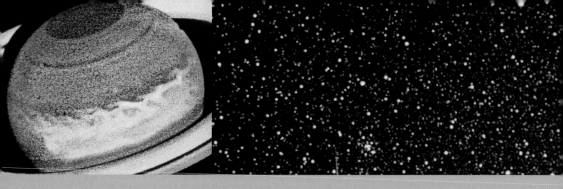

1684	Cassini discovers two more moons of Saturn, Tethys and Dione.
1789	British astronomer William Herschel announces that Saturn has two solid rings, discovers the moons Enceladus and Mimas, and observes that Saturn is flattened at its poles.
1837	German astronomer Johann Encke observes a dark band in the middle of the A ring, now known as Encke's Division.
1848	The moon Hyperion is discovered.
1856	James Clerk Maxwell realizes the rings of Saturn cannot be solid.
1857	Bright white spots are observed on Saturn.
1898	The moon Phoebe is discovered.
1957	The former Soviet Union (U.S.S.R.) launches *Sputnik 1*, the first artificial satellite.
1958	The first U.S. satellite, *Explorer 1*, is launched.

1959	— The Soviet Union's *Luna 1* probe to the Moon is launched, the first spacecraft to leave Earth orbit, opening the age of planetary exploration by spacecraft.
1960	— Scientists realize that Saturn's Great White Spot has a 30-year cycle.
1966	— The moon Janus is discovered.
1979	— *Pioneer 11* takes the first close look at Titan and the Saturn system.
1980	— *Voyager 1* flies by Saturn and its moons. The moons Atlas, Prometheus, Pandora, Epimetheus, and Helene are discovered.
1981	— *Voyager 2* flies by Saturn and its moons. The moons Telesto and Calypso are discovered sharing the orbit of Tethys.
1990	— The Great White Spot reappears in Saturn's atmosphere.

The moon Pan is discovered from Voyager images. |

1995	— The *Hubble Space Telescope* provides the first good close-up views of Titan.
1997	— *Cassini-Huygens* is launched and heads for Saturn and Titan.
1998	— *Cassini-Huygens* flies by Venus for the first of two gravity assists.
1999	— *Cassini-Huygens* flies by Jupiter.
2004	*Cassini-Huygens* is scheduled to arrive at Saturn and Titan.

Glossary

asteroid—a piece of rocky debris left over from the formation of the solar system. Most asteroids orbit the Sun in a belt between Mars and Jupiter.

astrology—the unsupported belief that the positions of planets and stars at the time of a person's birth influence his or her future

astronomy—the scientific study of the universe—matter in outer space—including the position, dynamics, and history of planets and stars

aurora (pl. aurorae)—a display of light caused by interaction between charged particles and a planet's magnetic field

crater—a rimmed basin or depression in the surface of a planet or moon caused by the impact of a meteorite.

density—the amount of a substance in a given volume

eccentric orbit—a highly elliptical, flattened orbit

elliptical—oval-shaped, a flattened circle

exobiologist—a scientist who studies the possibility of life on other worlds *gravitational field*—the region around an object that is affected by its gravitational pull

gravity assist—a maneuver in which a spacecraft circles an object in space and uses that object's gravitational pull to increase its acceleration

hydrocarbon—a compound composed of a carbon and hydrogen

magnetic field—the area surrounding a magnet that is affected by the magnet's attractive force. Some planets have magnetic properties and, therefore, have a magnetic field.

magnetosphere—the vast area around a planet that is filled with electrically charged particles and electromagnetic radiation. It is caused by the interaction of the planet's magnetic field and the solar wind

meteorite—a particle of dust or rock that strikes the surface of a planet or moon

meteoroid—a rocky or metallic object of relatively small size, usually once part of a comet or asteroid

nebula—the primitive cloud of gases and dust from which the Sun and the planets were created

nuclear fusion—a process that takes place in the core of the Sun and other stars, releasing enormous energy when two atoms of hydrogen combine to form helium

planetesimal—the precursor of a planet

planetologist—a specialist in the study of planets

radiation belt—an area surrounding a planet, such as Earth or Saturn, that interacts with particles from the Sun

radius—the distance from the outer edge of a round object, such as a planet, to its center

red giant—a relatively cool, very large, and highly luminous star

retrograde—describes an orbit that is east-to-west, or clockwise, in the opposite direction from the usual

revolution—a circular path, or orbit, around another object

satellite—a natural or human-made object that orbits a planet or an asteroid

solar wind—the rush of electrically charged particles emitted by the Sun

spectroscope—a device used to determine what an object in space is composed of by examining the spectrum it emits

tidal force—the difference between the force of gravity on the near and far sides of an object in space

ultraviolet radiation—wavelengths just shorter than those associated with visible light; "black light" is a form of UV radiation

To Find Out More

The news from space changes fast, so it's always a good idea to check the copyright date on books, CD-ROMs, and video tapes to make sure that you are getting up-to-date information. One good place to look for current information from NASA is U.S. government depository libraries. There are several in each state.

Books

Campbell, Ann Jeanette. *The New York Public Library Amazing Space: A Book of Answers for Kids.* New York: John Wiley & Sons, 1997.

Dickinson, Terence. *Other Worlds: A Beginner's Guide to Planets and Moons.* Willowdale, Ontario: Firefly Books, 1995.

Gustafson, John. *Planets, Moons, and Meteors.* New York: Julian Messner, 1992.

Hartmann, William K. and Don Miller. *The Grand Tour.* New York: Workman, 1993.

Vogt, Gregory L. *The Solar System: Facts and Exploration.* New York: Twenty-First Century Books, 1995.

CD-ROMs

Beyond Planet Earth, Discovery Channel School, P.O. Box 970, Oxon Hill, MD 20750-0970.
An interactive journey to the planets, including Saturn. Includes video footage and more than 200 still photographs.

Video Tape

Discover Magazine: Solar System, Discovery Channel School, P.O. Box 970, Oxon Hill, MD 20750-0970

Organizations and Online Sites

These organizations and online sites are good sources of information about Saturn and the rest of the solar system. Many of the online sites listed below are NASA sites, with links to many other interesting sources of information about the solar system. You can also sign up to receive NASA news on many subjects via e-mail.

Astronomical Society of the Pacific
http://www.aspsky.org/
390 Ashton Avenue
San Francisco, CA 94112

The Astronomy Café

http://www2.ari.net/home/odenwald/cafe.html

This site answers questions and offers news and articles relating to astronomy and space. It is maintained by astronomer and NASA scientist Sten Odenwald.

NASA Ask a Space Scientist

http://image.gsfc.nasa.gov/poetry/ask/askmag.html#list

Take a look at the Interactive Page where NASA scientists answer your questions about astronomy, space, and space missions. The site also has access to archives and fact sheets.

NASA Newsroom

http://www.nasa.gov/newsinfo/newsroom.html

This site features NASA's latest press releases, status reports, and fact sheets. It includes a news archive with past reports and a search button for the NASA Web site. You can even sign up for e-mail versions of all NASA press releases.

The Nine Planets: A Multimedia Tour of the Solar System

http://www.seds.org/nineplanet/nineplanets/nineplanets.html

This site has excellent material on the planets, including Saturn. It was created and is maintained by the Students for the Exploration and Development of Space, University of Arizona.

Planetary Missions

http://nssdc.gsfc.nasa.gov/planetary/projects.html

At this site, you'll find NASA links to all current and past missions. It's a one-stop shopping center to a wealth of information.

The Planetary Society

http://www.planetary.org/

65 North Catalina Avenue
Pasadena, CA 91106-2301

Sky Online

http://www.skypub.com

This is the Web site for *Sky and Telescope* magazine and other publications of Sky Publishing Corporation. You'll find a good weekly news section on general space and astronomy news. The site also has tips for amateur astronomers as well as a nice selection of links. A list of science museums, planetariums, and astronomy clubs organized by state can help you locate nearby places to visit.

Welcome to the Planets

http://pds.jpl.nasa.gov/planets/

This tour of the solar system has lots of pictures and information. The site was created and is maintained by the California Institute of Technology for NASA/Jet Propulsion Laboratory.

Windows to the Universe
http://windows.ivv.nasa.gov/
This NASA site, developed by the University of Michigan, includes sections on "Our Planet," "Our Solar System," "Space Missions," and "Kids' Space." Choose from presentation levels of beginner, intermediate, or advanced.

Places to Visit

Check the Internet (*www.skypub.com* is a good place to start), your local visitor's center, or phone directory for planetariums and science museums near you. Here are a few other suggestions:

Ames Research Center
Moffett Field, CA 94035
http://www.arc.nasa.gov/
Located near Mountain View and Sunnyvale on the San Francisco Peninsula, Ames Research Center welcomes visitors. This is the branch of NASA that heads the search for extraterrestrial life. Drop-in visitors are welcome and admission is free.

Exploratorium
3601 Lyon Street
San Francisco, CA 94123
http://www.exploratorium.edu/
You'll find internationally acclaimed interactive science exhibits, including astronomy subjects.

Jet Propulsion Laboratory (JPL)
4800 Oak Grove Drive
Pasadena, CA 91109
JPL is the primary mission center for most NASA planetary missions.
Tours are available once or twice a week by arrangement.

National Air and Space Museum
7th and Independence Ave., S.W.
Washington, DC 20560
http://www.nasm.edu/NASMDOCS/VISIT/
This museum, located on the National Mall west of the Capitol building, has all kinds of interesting exhibits.

Bold numbers indicate illustrations.

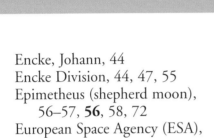

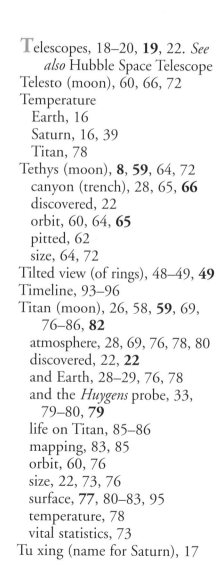

Ray Spangenburg and **Kit Moser** are a husband-and-wife writing team specializing in science and technology. They have written 38 books and more than 100 articles, including a 5-book series on the history of science and a 4-book series on the history of space exploration. As journalists, they covered NASA and related science activities for many years. They have flown on NASA's Kuiper Airborne Observatory, covered stories at the Deep Space Network in the Mojave Desert, and experienced zero-gravity on experimental NASA flights out of NASA Ames Research Center. They live in Carmichael, California, with their two dogs, Mencken (a Sharpei mix) and F. Scott Fitz (a Boston terrier).